RILEY SONGS OF HOME

RILEY
SONGS OF HOME

JAMES WHITCOMB RILEY

WITH PICTURES BY
WILL VAWTER

NEW YORK
GROSSET & DUNLAP
PUBLISHERS

TO
GEORGE A. CARR

CONTENTS

CONTENTS—Continued

RILEY SONGS OF HOME

WE MUST GET HOME

WE must get home! How could we stray like
      this?—
So far from home, we know not where it is,—
Only in some fair, apple-blossomy place
Of children's faces—and the mother's face—
We dimly dream it, till the vision clears
Even in the eyes of fancy, glad with tears.

19

We must get home—for we have been away
So long, it seems forever and a day!
And O so very homesick we have grown,
The laughter of the world is like a moan
In our tired hearing, and its song as vain,—
We must get home—we must get home again!

We must get home! With heart and soul we yearn
To find the long-lost pathway, and return! . . .
The child's shout lifted from the questing band
Of old folk, faring weary, hand in hand,
But faces brightening, as if clouds at last
Were showering sunshine on us as we passed.

We must get home: It hurts so staying here,
Where fond hearts must be wept out tear by tear,
And where to wear wet lashes means, at best,
When most our lack, the least our hope of rest—
When most our need of joy, the more our pain—
We must get home—we must get home again!

II

But yesterday!—
Adream, astray,
From morning's red to evening's gray,
O'er dales and hills
Of daffodills
And lorn sweet-fluting whippoorwills.

I knew nor cares
Nor tears nor prayers—
A mortal god, crowned unawares
With sunset—and
A scepter-wand
Of apple-blossoms in my hand!

The dewy blue
Of twilight grew
To purple, with a star or two
Whose lisping rays
Failed in the blaze
Of sudden fireflies through the haze.

We must get home—home to the simple things—
The morning-glories twirling up the strings
And bugling color, as they blared in blue-
And-white o'er garden-gates we scampered through;
The long grape-arbor, with its under-shade
Blue as the green and purple overlaid.

We must get home: All is so quiet there:
The touch of loving hands on brow and hair—
Dim rooms, wherein the sunshine is made mild—
The lost love of the mother and the child
Restored in restful lullabies of rain,—
We must get home—we must get home again!

The rows of sweetcorn and the China beans
Beyond the lettuce-beds where, towering, leans
The giant sunflower in barbaric pride
Guarding the barn-door and the lane outside;
The honeysuckles, midst the hollyhocks,
That clamber almost to the martin-box.

IV

But yesterday! . . .
O blooms of May,
And summer roses—where-away?
O stars above;
And lips of love,
And all the honeyed sweets thereof!—

O lad and lass,
And orchard pass,
And briered lane, and daisied grass!
O gleam and gloom,
And woodland bloom,
And breezy breaths of all perfume!—

No more for me
Or mine shall be
Thy raptures—save in memory,—
No more—no more—
Till through the Door
Of Glory gleam the days of yore.

JUST TO BE GOOD

JUST to be good—
        This is enough—enough!
O we who find sin's billows wild and rough,
Do we not feel how more than any gold
Would be the blameless life we led of old
While yet our lips knew but a mother's kiss?
        Ah! though we miss
        All else but this,
            To be good is enough!

It is enough—
        Enough—just to be good!
To lift our hearts where they are understood;
To let the thirst for worldly power and place
Go unappeased; to smile back in God's face
With the glad lips our mothers used to kiss.
        Ah! though we miss
        All else but this,
            To be good is enough!

OUR KIND OF A MAN

I

THE kind of a man for you and me!
    He faces the world unflinchingly,
And smites, as long as the wrong resists,
With a knuckled faith and force like fists:
He lives the life he is preaching of,
And loves where most is the need of love;
His voice is clear to the deaf man's ears,
And his face sublime through the blind man's tears;
The light shines out where the clouds were dim,
And the widow's prayer goes up for him;
The latch is clicked at the hovel door
And the sick man sees the sun once more,
And out o'er the barren fields he sees
Springing blossoms and waving trees,
Feeling as only the dying may,
That God's own servant has come that way,
Smoothing the path as it still winds on
Through the Golden Gate where his loved have gone.

II

The kind of a man for me and you!
However little of worth we do
He credits full, and abides in trust
That time will teach us how more is just.
He walks abroad, and he meets all kinds
Of querulous and uneasy minds,
And, sympathizing, he shares the pain
Of the doubts that rack us, heart and brain;
And, knowing this, as we grasp his hand,
We are surely coming to understand!
He looks on sin with pitying eyes—
E'en as the Lord, since Paradise,—
Else, should we read, "Though our sins should glow
As scarlet, they shall be white as snow"?—
And, feeling still, with a grief half glad,
That the bad are as good as the good are bad,
He strikes straight out for the Right—and he
Is the kind of a man for you and me!

MY FRIEND

"He is my friend!" The words
Brought summer and the birds;
And all my winter-time
Thawed into running rhyme
And rippled into song,
Warm, tender, brave and strong.

And so it sings to-day.—
So may it sing alway!
Though waving grasses grow
Between, and lilies blow
Their trills of perfume clear
As laughter to the ear,
Let each mute measure end
With "Still he is thy friend."

THINKIN' BACK

I 'VE ben thinkin' back, of late,
S'prisin'!—And I'm here to state
I'm suspicious it's a sign
Of *age,* maybe, er decline
Of my faculties,—and yit
I'm not *feelin'* old a bit—
Any more than sixty-four
Ain't no *young* man any more!

31

Us young-uns used to grin,
    At breakfast, on the sly,
And mock the wobble of his chin
    And eyebrows helt so high
And kind: *"How did you rest, last night?"*
    We'd mumble and let on
Our voices trimbled, and our sight
    Was dim, and hearin' gone.

o   •   •   •   •   •   ə   •   •   o

Bad as I used to be,
    All I'm a-wantin' is
As puore and ca'm a sleep fer me
    And sweet a sleep as his!
And so I pray, on Jedgment Day
    To wake, and with its light
See *his* face dawn, and hear him say—
    "How did you rest, last night?"

Thinkin' back, I even hear
Them a-callin', high and clear,
Up the crick-banks, where they seem
Still hid in there—like a dream—
And me still a-pantin' on
The green pathway they have gone!
Still they hide, by bend er ford—
Still they hide—but, thank the Lord,
(Thinkin' back, as I have said),
I hear laughin' on ahead!

JACK-IN-THE-BOX

(Grandfather, musing.)

IN childish days! O memory,
You bring such curious things to me!—
Laughs to the lip—tears to the eye,
In looking on the gifts that lie
Like broken playthings scattered o'er
Imagination's nursery floor!
Did these old hands once click the key
That let "Jack's" box-lid upward fly,
And that blear-eyed, fur-whiskered elf
Leap, as though frightened at himself,
And quiveringly lean and stare
At me, his jailer, laughing there?

We are not always glad when we smile!—
   But the conscience is quick to record,
     All the sorrow and sin
     We are hiding within
   Is plain in the sight of the Lord:
And ever, O ever, till pride
   And evasion shall cease to defile
     The sacred recess
     Of the soul, we confess
We are not always glad when we smile.

37

HIS ROOM

"I 'M home again, my dear old Room,
    I'm home again, and happy, too,
As, peering through the brightening gloom,
    I find myself alone with you:
        Though brief my stay, nor far away,
        I missed you—missed you night and day—
        As wildly yearned for you as now.—
        Old Room, how are you, anyhow?

"My easy chair, with open arms,
    Awaits me just within the door;
The littered carpet's woven charms
    Have never seemed so bright before,—
        The old rosettes and mignonettes
        And ivy-leaves and violets,
        Look up as pure and fresh of hue
        As though baptized in morning dew.

"Old Room, to me your homely walls
    Fold round me like the arms of love,
And over all my being falls
    A blessing pure as from above—
        Even as a nestling child caressed
        And lulled upon a loving breast,
        With folded eyes, too glad to weep
        And yet too sad for dreams or sleep.

"You've been so kind to me, old Room—
    So patient in your tender care,
My drooping heart in fullest bloom
    Has blossomed for you unaware;
        And who but you had cared to woo
        A heart so dark, and heavy, too,
        As in the past you lifted mine
        From out the shadow to the shine?

"For I was but a wayward boy
    When first you gladly welcomed me
And taught me work was truer joy
    Than rioting incessantly:
        And thus the din that stormed within
        The old guitar and violin
        Has fallen in a fainter tone
        And sweeter, for your sake alone.

39

"Though in my absence I have stood
  In festal halls a favored guest,
I missed, in this old quietude,
  My worthy work and worthy rest—
    By *this* I know that long ago
    You loved me first, and told me so
    In art's mute eloquence of speech
    The voice of praise may never reach.

"For lips and eyes in truth's disguise
  Confuse the faces of my friends,
Till old affection's fondest ties
  I find unraveling at the ends;
    But as I turn to you, and learn
    To meet my griefs with less concern,
    Your love seems all I have to keep
    Me smiling lest I needs must weep.

"Yet I am happy, and would fain
  Forget the world and all its woes;
So set me to my tasks again,
  Old Room, and lull me to repose:
    And as we glide adown the tide
    Of dreams, forever side by side,
    I'll hold your hands as lovers do
    Their sweethearts' and talk love to you."

THE PLAINT HUMAN

SEASON of snows, and season of flowers,
    Seasons of loss and gain!—
Since grief and joy must alike be ours,
    Why do we still complain?

Ever our failing, from sun to sun,
    O my intolerant brother—
We want just a little too little of one,
    And much too much of the other.

43

THE QUEST

I AM looking for Love. Has he passed this way,
  With eyes as blue as the skies of May,
And a face as fair as the summer dawn?—
You answer back, but I wander on,—
For you say: "Oh, yes; but his eyes were gray,
And his face as dim as a rainy day."

Good friends, I query, I search for Love;
His eyes are as blue as the skies above,
And his smile as bright as the midst of May
When the truce-bird pipes: Has he passed this
        way?
And one says: "Ay; but his face, alack!
Frowned as he passed, and his eyes were black."

O who will tell me of Love? I cry!
His eyes are as blue as the mid-May sky,
And his face as bright as the morning sun;
And you answer and mock me, every one,
That his eyes were dark, and his face was wan,
And he passed you frowning and wandered on.

44

But stout of heart will I onward fare,
Knowing *my* Love is beyond—somewhere,—
The Love I seek, with the eyes of blue,
And the bright, sweet smile unknown of you;
And on from the hour his trail is found
I shall sing sonnets the whole year round.

THE MULBERRY TREE

O IT'S many's the scenes which is dear to my
           mind
As I think of my childhood so long left behind;
The home of my birth, with it's old puncheon-floor,
And the bright morning-glories that growed round the
           door;
The warped clab-board roof whare the rain it run off
Into streams of sweet dreams as I laid in the loft,
Countin' all of the joys that was dearest to me,
And a-thinkin' the most of the mulberry tree.

And to-day as I dream, with both eyes wide-awake,
I can see the old tree, and its limbs as they shake,
And the long purple berries that rained on the ground
Whare the pastur' was bald whare we trommpt it
           around.
And again, peekin' up through the thick leafy shade,
I can see the glad smiles of the friends when I strayed
With my little bare feet from my own mother's knee
To foller them off to the mulberry tree.

46

Leanin' up in the forks, I can see the old rail,
And the boy climbin' up it, claw, tooth, and toe-nail,
And in fancy can hear, as he spits on his hands,
The ring of his laugh and the rip of his pants.
But that rail led to glory, as certin and shore
As I'll never climb thare by that rout' any more—
What was all the green lauruls of Fame unto me,
With my brows in the boughs of the mulberry tree!

Then it's who can fergit the old mulberry tree
That he knowed in the days when his thoughts was as
        free
As the flutterin' wings of the birds that flew out
Of the tall wavin' tops as the boys come about?
O, a crowd of my memories, laughin' and gay,
Is a-climbin' the fence of that pastur' to-day,
And, a-pantin' with joy, as us boys ust to be,
They go racin' acrost fer the mulberry tree.

FOR YOU

FOR you, I could forget the gay
   Delirium of merriment,
And let my laughter die away
  In endless silence of content.
    I could forget, for your dear sake,
    The utter emptiness and ache
    Of every loss I ever knew.—
    What could I not forget for you?

FOR YOU

I could forget the just deserts
 Of mine own sins, and so erase
The tear that burns, the smile that hurts,
 And all that mars or masks my face.
  For your fair sake I could forget
  The bonds of life that chafe and fret,
  Nor care if death were false or true.—
  What could I not forget for you?

What could I not forget? Ah me!
 One thing, I know, would still abide
Forever in my memory,
 Though all of love were lost beside—
  I yet would feel how first the wine
  Of your sweet lips made fools of mine
  Until they sung, all drunken through—
  "What could I not forget for you?"

51

A FEEL IN THE CHRIS'MAS-AIR

THEY'S a kind o' *feel* in the air, to me,
    When the Chris'mas-times sets in,
That's about as much of a mystery
    As ever I've run ag'in!—
Fer instunce, now, whilse I gain in weight
    And gineral health, I swear
They's a *goneness* somers I can't quite state—
    A kind o' *feel* in the air.

They's a feel in the Chris'mas-air goes right
  To the spot where a man *lives* at!—
It gives a feller a' appetite—
  They ain't no doubt about *that!*—
And yit they's *somepin'*—I don't know what—
  That follers me, here and there,
And ha'nts and worries and spares me not—
  A kind o' feel in the air!

They's a *feel,* as I say, in the air that's jest
  As blame-don sad as sweet!—
In the same ra-sho as I feel the best
  And am spryest on my feet,
They's allus a kind o' sort of a' *ache*
  That I can't lo-cate no-where;—
But it comes with *Chris'mas,* and no mistake!—
  A kind o' feel in the air.

Is it the racket the childern raise?—
  W'y, *no!*—God bless 'em!—*no!*—
Is it the eyes and the cheeks ablaze—
  Like my *own* wuz, long ago?—
Is it the bleat o' the whistle and beat
  O' the little toy-drum and blare
O' the horn?—*No! no!*—it is jest the sweet—
  The sad-sweet feel in the air.

AS CREATED

THERE'S a space for good to bloom in
  Every heart of man or woman,—
And however wild or human,
  Or however brimmed with gall,
Never heart may beat without it;
And the darkest heart to doubt it
Has something good about it
              After all.

WHERE-AWAY

O THE Lands of Where-Away!
   Tell us—tell us—where are they?
Through the darkness and the dawn
We have journeyed on and on—
From the cradle to the cross—
From possession unto loss.—
Seeking still, from day to day,
For the Lands of Where-Away.

When our baby-feet were first
Planted where the daisies burst,
And the greenest grasses grew
In the fields we wandered through,—
On, with childish discontent,
Ever on and on we went,
Hoping still to pass, some day,
O'er the verge of Where-Away.

Roses laid their velvet lips
On our own, with fragrant sips;
But their kisses held us not,
All their sweetness we forgot;—
Though the brambles in our track
Plucked at us to hold us back—
"Just ahead," we used to say,
"Lie the Lands of Where-Away."

Children at the pasture-bars,
Through the dusk, like glimmering stars,
Waved their hands that we should bide
With them over eventide;
Down the dark their voices failed
Falteringly, as they hailed,
And died into yesterday—
Night ahead and—Where-Away?

Twining arms about us thrown—
Warm caresses, all our own,
Can but stay us for a spell—
Love hath little new to tell
To the soul in need supreme,
Aching ever with the dream
Of the endless bliss it may
Find in Lands of Where-Away!

58

DREAMER, SAY

DREAMER, say, will you dream for me
   A wild sweet dream of a foreign land,
Whose border sips of a foaming sea
   With lips of coral and silver sand;
Where warm winds loll on the shady deeps,
   Or lave themselves in the tearful mist
The great wild wave of the breaker weeps
   O'er crags of opal and amethyst?

DREAMER, SAY

Dreamer, say, will you dream a dream
   Of tropic shades in the lands of shine,
Where the lily leans o'er an amber stream
   That flows like a rill of wasted wine,—
Where the palm-trees, lifting their shields of green,
   Parry the shafts of the Indian sun
Whose splintering vengeance falls between
   The reeds below where the waters run?

Dreamer, say, will you dream of love
   That lives in a land of sweet perfume,
Where the stars drip down from the skies above
   In molten spatters of bud and bloom?
Where never the weary eyes are wet,
   And never a sob in the balmy air,
And only the laugh of the paroquette
   Breaks the sleep of the silence there?

OUR OWN

THEY walk here with us, hand-in-hand;
　　We gossip, knee-by-knee;
They tell us all that they have planned—
　　Of all their joys to be,—
And, laughing, leave us:　And, to-day,
　　All desolate we cry
Across wide waves of voiceless graves—
　　Good-by!　Good-by!　Good-by!

THE OLD TRUNDLE-BED

O THE old trundle-bed where I slept when a boy!
    What canopied king might not covet the joy?
The glory and peace of that slumber of mine,
Like a long, gracious rest in the bosom divine:
The quaint, homely couch, hidden close from the light,
But daintily drawn from its hiding at night.
O a nest of delight, from the foot to the head,
Was the queer little, dear little, old trundle-bed!

O the old trundle-bed, where I wondering saw
The stars through the window, and listened with awe
To the sigh of the winds as they tremblingly crept
Through the trees where the robin so restlessly slept:
Where I heard the low, murmurous chirp of the wren,
And the katydid listlessly chirrup again,
Till my fancies grew faint and were drowsily led
Through the maze of the dreams of the old trundle-
      bed.

O the old trundle-bed! O the old trundle-bed!
With its plump little pillow, and old-fashioned spread;
Its snowy-white sheets, and the blankets above,
Smoothed down and tucked round with the touches of
      love;
The voice of my mother to lull me to sleep
With the old fairy-stories my memories keep
Still fresh as the lilies that bloom o'er the head
Once bowed o'er my own in the old trundle-bed.

WHO BIDES HIS TIME

WHO bides his time, and day by day
    Faces defeat full patiently,
And lifts a mirthful roundelay,
    However poor his fortunes be,—
He will not fail in any qualm
    Of poverty—the paltry dime
It will grow golden in his palm,
    Who bides his time.

WHO BIDES HIS TIME

Who bides his time—he tastes the sweet
　Of honey in the saltest tear;
And though he fares with slowest feet,
　Joy runs to meet him, drawing near;
The birds are heralds of his cause;
　And, like a never-ending rhyme,
The roadsides bloom in his applause,
　　　Who bides his time.

Who bides his time, and fevers not
　In the hot race that none achieves,
Shall wear cool-wreathen laurel, wrought
　With crimson berries in the leaves;
And he shall reign a goodly king,
　And sway his hand o'er every clime,
With peace writ on his signet-ring,
　　　Who bides his time.

NATURAL PERVERSITIES

I AM not prone to moralize
   In scientific doubt
On certain facts that Nature tries
   To puzzle us about,—
For I am no philosopher
   Of wise elucidation,
But speak of things as they occur,
   From simple observation.

I notice *little* things—to wit :—
   I never missed a train
Because I didn't *run* for it;
   I never knew it rain
That my umbrella wasn't lent,—
   Or, when in my possession,
The sun but wore, to all intent,
   A jocular expression.

I never knew a creditor
  To dun me for a debt
But I was "cramped" or "busted;" or
  I never knew one yet,
When I had plenty in my purse,
  To make the least invasion,—
As I, accordingly perverse,
  Have courted no occasion.

Nor do I claim to comprehend
  What Nature has in view
In giving us the very friend
  To trust we oughtn't to.—
But so it is: The trusty gun
  Disastrously exploded
Is always sure to be the one
  We didn't think was loaded.

Our moaning is another's mirth,—
  And what is worse by half,
We say the funniest thing on earth
  And never raise a laugh:
Mid friends that love us overwell,
  And sparkling jests and liquor,
Our hearts somehow are liable
  To melt in tears the quicker.

73

We reach the wrong when most we seek
  The right; in like effect,
We stay the strong and not the weak—
  Do most when we neglect.—
Neglected genius—truth be said—
  As wild and quick as tinder,
The more we seek to help ahead
  The more we seem to hinder.

I've known the least the greatest, too—
  And, on the selfsame plan,
The biggest fool I ever knew
  Was quite a little man:
We find we ought, and then we won't—
  We prove a thing, then doubt it,—
Know *everything* but when we don't
  Know *anything* about it.

A SCRAWL

I WANT to sing something—but this is all—
  I try and I try, but the rhymes are dull
As though they were damp, and the echoes fall
  Limp and unlovable.

Words will not say what I yearn to say—
  They will not walk as I want them to,
But they stumble and fall in the path of the way
  Of my telling my love for you.

Simply take what the scrawl is worth—-
  Knowing I love you as sun the sod
On the ripening side of the great round earth
  That swings in the smile of God.

75

WRITIN' BACK TO THE HOME-FOLKS

MY dear old friends—It jes beats all,
  The way you write a letter
So's ever' *last* line beats the *first,*
  And ever' *next*-un's better!—
W'y, ever' fool-thing you putt down
  You make so int*erest*in',
A feller, readin' of 'em all,
  Can't tell which is the *best*-un.

It's all so comfortin' and good,
  'Pears-like I almost *hear* ye
And git more sociabler, you know,
  And hitch my cheer up near ye
And jes smile on ye like the sun
  Acrosst the whole per-rairies
In Aprile when the thaw's begun
  And country couples marries.

It's all so good-old-fashioned like
  To *talk* jes like we're *thinkin'*,
Without no hidin' back o' fans
  And giggle-un and winkin',
Ner sizin' how each-other's dressed—
  Like some is allus doin',—
"*Is* Marthy Ellen's basque ben *turned*
  Er shore-enough a new-un!"—

Er "ef Steve's city-friend haint jes
  'A *lee*tle kindo'-sorto' "—
Er "wears them-air blame eye-glasses
  Jes 'cause he hadn't ort to?"
And so straight on, *dad-libitum*,
  Tel all of us feels, *some*way,
Jes like our "comp'ny" wuz the best
  When we git up to come 'way!

That's why I like *old* friends like you,—
  Jes 'cause you're so *abidin'*.—
Ef I was built to live *"fer keeps,"*
  My principul residin'
Would be amongst the folks 'at kep'
  Me allus *thinkin'* of 'em,
And sorto' eechin' all the time
  To tell 'em how I love 'em.—

79

Sich folks, you know, I jes love so
    I wouldn't live without 'em,
Er couldn't even drap asleep
    But what I *dreamp'* about 'em,—
And ef we minded God, I guess
    We'd *all* love one-another
Jes like one fam'bly,—me and Pap
    And Madaline and Mother.

LAUGHTER HOLDING BOTH HIS SIDES

A Y, thou varlet!—Laugh away!
   All the world's a holiday!
Laugh away, and roar and shout
Till thy hoarse tongue lolleth out!
Bloat thy cheeks, and bulge thine eyes
Unto bursting; pelt thy thighs
With thy swollen palms, and roar
As thou never hast before!
Lustier! wilt thou! peal on peal!
Stiflest? Squat and grind thy heel—
Wrestle with thy loins, and then
Wheeze thee whiles, and whoop again!

THE SONG OF YESTERDAY

I

BUT yesterday
I looked away
O'er happy lands, where sunshine lay
In golden blots
Inlaid with spots
Of shade and wild forget-me-nots.

My head was fair
With flaxen hair,
And fragrant breezes, faint and rare,
And warm with drouth
From out the south,
Blew all my curls across my mouth.

And, cool and sweet,
My naked feet
Found dewy pathways through the wheat;
And out again
Where, down the lane,
The dust was dimpled with the rain.

II

But yesterday!—
Adream, astray,
From morning's red to evening's gray,
O'er dales and hills
Of daffodills
And lorn sweet-fluting whippoorwills.

I knew nor cares
Nor tears nor prayers—
A mortal god, crowned unawares
With sunset—and
A scepter-wand
Of apple-blossoms in my hand!

The dewy blue
Of twilight grew
To purple, with a star or two
Whose lisping rays
Failed in the blaze
Of sudden fireflies through the haze.

III

But yesterday
I heard the lay
Of summer birds, when I, as they
With breast and wing,
All quivering
With life and love, could only sing.

My head was lent
Where, with it, blent
A maiden's o'er her instrument;
While all the night,
From vale to height,
Was filled with echoes of delight.

And all our dreams
Were lit with gleams
Of that lost land of reedy streams,
Along whose brim
Forever swim
Pan's lilies, laughing up at him.

IV

But yesterday! . . .
O blooms of May,
And summer roses—where-away?
O stars above;
And lips of love,
And all the honeyed sweets thereof!—

O lad and lass,
And orchard pass,
And briered lane, and daisied grass!
O gleam and gloom,
And woodland bloom,
And breezy breaths of all perfume!—

No more for me
Or mine shall be
Thy raptures—save in memory,—
No more—no more—
Till through the Door
Of Glory gleam the days of yore.

SONG OF PARTING

SAY farewell, and let me go;
   Shatter every vow!
All the future can bestow
   Will be welcome now!
     And if this fair hand I touch
     I have worshipped overmuch,
     It was my mistake—and so,
     Say farewell, and let me go.

Say farewell, and let me go:
   Murmur no regret,
Stay your tear-drops ere they flow—
   Do not waste them yet!
      They might pour as pours the rain,
      And not wash away the pain:
      I have tried them and I know.—
      Say farewell, and let me go.

Say farewell, and let me go:
   Think me not untrue—
True as truth is, even so
   I am true to you!
      If the ghost of love may stay
      Where my fond heart dies to-day,
      I am with you alway—so,
      Say farewell, and let me go.

OUR KIND OF A MAN

I

THE kind of a man for you and me!
  He faces the world unflinchingly,
And smites, as long as the wrong resists,
With a knuckled faith and force like fists:
He lives the life he is preaching of,
And loves where most is the need of love;
His voice is clear to the deaf man's ears,
And his face sublime through the blind man's tears;
The light shines out where the clouds were dim,
And the widow's prayer goes up for him;
The latch is clicked at the hovel door
And the sick man sees the sun once more,
And out o'er the barren fields he sees
Springing blossoms and waving trees,
Feeling as only the dying may,
That God's own servant has come that way,
Smoothing the path as it still winds on
Through the Golden Gate where his loved have gone.

II

The kind of a man for me and you!
However little of worth we do
He credits full, and abides in trust
That time will teach us how more is just.
He walks abroad, and he meets all kinds
Of querulous and uneasy minds,
And, sympathizing, he shares the pain
Of the doubts that rack us, heart and brain;
And, knowing this, as we grasp his hand,
We are surely coming to understand!
He looks on sin with pitying eyes—
E'en as the Lord, since Paradise,—
Else, should we read, "Though our sins should glow
As scarlet, they shall be white as snow"?—
And, feeling still, with a grief half glad,
That the bad are as good as the good are bad,
He strikes straight out for the Right—and he
Is the kind of a man for you and me!

"HOW DID YOU REST, LAST NIGHT?"

"HOW did you rest, last night?"—
    I've heard my gran'pap say
Them words a thousand times—that's right—
    Jes them words thataway!
As punctchul-like as morning dast
    To ever heave in sight
Gran'pap 'ud allus haf to ast—
    "How did you rest, last night?"

Us young-uns used to grin,
　At breakfast, on the sly,
And mock the wobble of his chin
　And eyebrows helt so high
And kind: *"How did you rest, last night?"*
　We'd mumble and let on
Our voices trimbled, and our sight
　Was dim, and hearin' gone.

·　·　·　·　·　·　·　·　·　·

Bad as I used to be,
　All I'm a-wantin' is
As puore and ca'm a sleep fer me
　And sweet a sleep as his!
And so I pray, on Jedgment Day
　To wake, and with its light
See *his* face dawn, and hear him say—
　"How did you rest, last night?"

OUT OF THE HITHERWHERE

OUT of the hitherwhere into the Yon—
    The land that the Lord's love rests upon;
Where one may rely on the friends he meets,
And the smiles that greet him along the streets:
Where the mother that left you years ago
Will lift the hands that were folded so,
And put them about you, with all the love
And tenderness you are dreaming of.

98

Out of the hitherwhere into the Yon—
Where all of the friends of your youth have gone,—
Where the old schoolmate that laughed with you,
Will laugh again as he used to do,
Running to meet you, with such a face
As lights like a moon the wondrous place
Where God is living, and glad to live,
Since He is the Master and may forgive.

Out of the hitherwhere into the Yon!—
Stay the hopes we are leaning on—
You, Divine, with Your merciful eyes
Looking down from the far-away skies,—
Smile upon us, and reach and take
Our worn souls Home for the old home's sake.—
And so Amen,—for our all seems gone
Out of the hitherwhere into the Yon.

JACK-IN-THE-BOX

(Grandfather, musing.)

IN childish days! O memory,
You bring such curious things to me!—
Laughs to the lip—tears to the eye,
In looking on the gifts that lie
Like broken playthings scattered o'er
Imagination's nursery floor!
Did these old hands once click the key
That let "Jack's" box-lid upward fly,
And that blear-eyed, fur-whiskered elf
Leap, as though frightened at himself,
And quiveringly lean and stare
At me, his jailer, laughing there?

A child then! Now—I only know
They call me very old; and so
They will not let me have my way,—
But uselessly I sit all day
Here by the chimney-jamb, and poke
The lazy fire, and smoke and smoke,
And watch the wreaths swoop up the flue,
And chuckle—ay, I often do—
Seeing again, all vividly,
Jack-in-the-box leap, as in glee
To see how much he looks like me!

. . . They talk. I can't hear what they say—
But I am glad, clean through and through
Sometimes, in fancying that they
Are saying, "Sweet, that fancy strays
In age back to our childish days!"

THE BOYS

WHERE are they?—the friends of my childhood
          enchanted—
The clear, laughing eyes looking back in my own,
And the warm, chubby fingers my palms have so
        wanted,
  As when we raced over
        Pink pastures of clover,
And mocked the quail's whir and the bumblebee's
        drone?

Have the breezes of time blown their blossomy faces
  Forever adrift down the years that are flown?
Am I never to see them romp back to their places,
  Where over the meadow,
        In sunshine and shadow,
The meadow-larks trill, and the bumblebees drone?

Where are they? Ah! dim in the dust lies the clover;
  The whippoorwill's call has a sorrowful tone,
And the dove's—I have wept at it over and over;—
  I want the glad luster
        Of youth, and the cluster
Of faces asleep where the bumblebees drone!

IT'S *GOT* TO BE

"WHEN it's *got* to be,"—like I always say,
　　As I notice the years whiz past,
And know each day is a yesterday,
　　When we size it up, at last,—
Same as I said when my *boyhood* went
　　And I knowed *we* had to quit,—
"It's *got* to be, and it's *goin'* to be!"—
　　So I said "Good-by" to *it*.

It's *got* to be, and it's *goin'* to be!
　　So at least I always try
To kind o' say in a hearty way,—
　　"Well, it's *got* to be.　Good-by!"

The time jes melts like a late, last snow,—
    When it's *got* to be, it melts!
But I aim to keep a cheerful mind,
    Ef I can't keep nothin' else!
I knowed, when I come to twenty-one,
    That I'd soon be twenty-two,—
So I waved one hand at the soft young man,
    And I said, "Good-by to *you!*"

It's *got* to be, and it's *goin'* to be!
    So at least I always try
To kind o' say, in a cheerful way,—
    "Well, it's *got* to be.—Good-by!"

They kep' a-goin', the years and years,
    Yet still I smiled and smiled,—
For I'd said "Good-by" to my single life,
    And I now had a wife and child:
Mother and son and the father—one,—
    Till, last, on her bed of pain,
She jes' smiled up, like she always done,—
    And I said "Good-by" again.

It's *got* to be, and it's *goin'* to be!
    So at least I always try
To kind o' say, in a humble way,—
    "Well, it's *got* to be. Good-by!"

And then my boy—as he growed to be
   Almost a man in size,—
Was more than a pride and joy to me,
   With his mother's smilin' eyes.—
He gimme the slip, when the War broke out,
   And followed me. And I
Never knowed till the first fight's end . . .
   I found him, and then, . . . "Good-by."

It's *got* to be, and it's *goin'* to be!
   So at least I always try
To kind o' say, in a patient way,
   "Well, it's *got* to be. Good-by!"

I have said, "Good-by!—Good-by!—Good-by!"
   With my very best good will,
All through life from the first,—and I
   Am a cheerful old man still:
But it's *got* to end, and it's *goin'* to end!
   And this is the thing I'll do,—
With my last breath I will laugh, O Death,
   And say "Good-by" to *you!* . . .

It's *got* to be! And again I say,—
   When his old scythe circles high,
I'll laugh—of course, in the kindest way,—
   As I say "Good-by!—Good-by!"

"OUT OF REACH?"

Y OU think them "out of reach," your dead?
  Nay, by my own dead, I deny
Your "out of reach."—Be comforted:
  'Tis not so far to die.

O by their dear remembered smiles
  And outheld hands and welcoming speech,
They wait for us, thousands of miles
  This side of "out-of-reach."

"A BRAVE REFRAIN"

WHEN snow is here, and the trees look weird,
    And the knuckled twigs are gloved with frost;
When the breath congeals in the drover's beard,
    And the old pathway to the barn is lost;
When the rooster's crow is sad to hear,
    And the stamp of the stabled horse is vain,
And the tone of the cow-bell grieves the ear—
    O then is the time for a brave refrain!

113

When the gears hang stiff on the harness-peg,
   And the tallow gleams in frozen streaks;
And the old hen stands on a lonesome leg,
   And the pump sounds hoarse and the handle squeaks;
When the woodpile lies in a shrouded heap,
   And the frost is scratched from the window-pane
And anxious eyes from the inside peep—
   O then is the time for a brave refrain!

When the ax-helve warms at the chimney-jamb,
   And hob-nailed shoes on the hearth below,
And the house-cat curls in a slumber calm,
   And the eight-day clock ticks loud and slow;
When the harsh broom-handle jabs the ceil
   'Neath the kitchen-loft, and the drowsy brain
Sniffs the breath of the morning meal—
   O then is the time for a brave refrain!

ENVOI

When the skillet seethes, and a blubbering hot
Tilts the lid of the coffee-pot,
And the scent of the buckwheat cake grows plain—
O then is the time for a brave refrain!

IN THE EVENING

I

IN the evening of our days,
  When the first far stars above
Glimmer dimmer, through the haze,
  Than the dewy eyes of love,
Shall we mournfully revert
  To the vanished morns and Mays
Of our youth, with hearts that hurt,—
  In the evening of our days?

II

Shall the hand that holds your own
　　Till the twain are thrilled as now,
Be withheld, or colder grown?
　　Shall my kiss upon your brow
Falter from its high estate?
　　And, in all forgetful ways,
Shall we sit apart and wait—
　　In the evening of our days?

III

Nay, my wife—my life!—the gloom
　　Shall enfold us velvetwise,
And my smile shall be the groom
　　Of the gladness of your eyes:
Gently, gently as the dew
　　Mingles with the darkening maze,
I shall fall asleep with you—
　　In the evening of our days.

JIM

HE was jes a plain, ever'-day, all-round kind of a
      jour.,
    Consumpted-lookin'—but la!
The jokiest, wittiest, story-tellin', song-singin', laugh-
    in'est, jolliest
    Feller you ever saw!
Worked at jes coarse work, but you kin bet he was fine
    enough in his talk,
    And his feelin's, too!
Lordy! ef he was on'y back on his bench ag'in to-day,
    a-carryin' on
    Like he ust to do!

Any shop-mate'll tell you there never was, on top o'
      dirt,
    A better feller'n Jim!
You want a favor, and couldn't git it anywheres else—
    You could git it o' him!
Most free-heartedest man thataway in the world, I
      guess!
    Give up ever' nickel he's worth—
And, ef you'd a-wanted it, and named it to him, and it
      was his,
    He'd a-give you the earth!

Allus a-reachin' out, Jim was, and a-he'ppin' some
    Pore feller onto his feet—
He'd a-never a-keered how hungry he was hisse'f,
    So's *the feller* got somepin' to eat!
Didn't make no differ'nce at all to him how *he* was
      dressed,
    He ust to say to me,—
"You togg out a tramp purty comfortable in winter-
      time, a-huntin' a job,
    And he'll git along!" says he.

Jim didn't have, ner never could git ahead, so overly
    much
    O' this world's goods at a time.—
'Fore now I've saw him, more'n onc't, lend a dollar,
    and haf to, more'n like,
    Turn round and borry a dime!
Mebby laugh and joke about it hisse'f fer a while—
    then jerk his coat,
    And kindo' square his chin,
Tie on his apern, and squat hisse'f on his old shoe-
    bench,
    And go to peggin' ag'in!

Patientest feller, too, I reckon, 'at ever jes natchurly
    Coughed hisse'f to death!
Long enough after his voice was lost he'd laugh in a
    whisper and say
    He could git ever'thing but his breath—
"*You* fellers," he'd sorto' twinkle his eyes and say,
    "Is a-pilin' onto me
A mighty big debt fer that-air little weak-chested ghost
    o' mine to pack
    Through all Eternity!"

Now there was a man 'at jes 'peared-like, to me,
   'At ortn't *a-never* a-died!
"But death hain't a-showin' no favors," the old boss
      said—
   "On'y to *Jim!*" and cried:
And Wigger, who puts up the best sewed-work in the
      shop—
   Er the whole blame neighborhood,—
He says, "When God made Jim, I bet you He didn't do
      anything else that day
   But jes set around and feel good!"

THE BEST IS GOOD ENOUGH

I QUARREL not with Destiny,
But make the best of everything—
The best is good enough for me.

Leave Discontent alone, and she
Will shut her mouth and let *you* sing.
I quarrel not with Destiny.

I take some things, or let 'em be—
Good gold has always got the ring;
The best is good enough for me.

THE BEST IS GOOD ENOUGH

Since Fate insists on secrecy,
I have no arguments to bring—
I quarrel not with Destiny.

The fellow that goes "haw" for "gee"
Will find he hasn't got full swing.
The best is good enough for me.

One only knows our needs, and He
Does all of the distributing.
I quarrel not with Destiny;
The best is good enough for me.

HONEY DRIPPING FROM THE COMB

H OW slight a thing may set one's fancy drifting
    Upon the dead sea of the Past!—A view—
Sometimes an odor—or a rooster lifting
    A far-off *"Ooh! ooh-ooh!"*

And suddenly we find ourselves astray
    In some wood's-pasture of the Long Ago—
Or idly dream again upon a day
    Of rest we used to know.

I bit an apple but a moment since—
    A wilted apple that the worm had spurned.—
Yet hidden in the taste were happy hints
    Of good old days returned.—

And so my heart, like some enraptured lute,
    Tinkles a tune so tender and complete,
God's blessing must be resting on the fruit—
    So bitter, yet so sweet!

AS MY UNCLE USED TO SAY

I'VE thought a power on men and things,
   As my uncle ust to say,—
And ef folks don't work as they pray, i jings!
   W'y, they ain't no use to pray!
Ef you want somepin', and jes dead-set
A-pleadin' fer it with both eyes wet,
And *tears* won't bring it, w'y, you try *sweat*,
   As my uncle ust to say.

They's some don't know their A, B, C's,
   As my uncle ust to say,
And yit don't waste no candle-grease,
   Ner whistle their lives away!
But ef they can't write no book, ner rhyme
No singin' song fer to last all time,
They can blaze the way fer the march sublime,
   As my uncle ust to say.

Whoever's Foreman of all things here,
    As my uncle ust to say,
He knows each job 'at we're best fit fer,
    And our round-up, night and day:
And a-sizin' *His* work, east and west,
And north and south, and worst and best.
I ain't got nothin' to suggest,
    As my uncle ust to say.

WE MUST BELIEVE

"Lord, I believe: help Thou mine unbelief."

WE must believe—
    Being from birth endowed with love and trust—
Born unto loving;—and how simply just
That love—that faith!—even in the blossom-face
The babe drops dreamward in its resting-place,
Intuitively conscious of the sure
Awakening to rapture ever pure
And sweet and saintly as the mother's own,
Or the awed father's, as his arms are thrown
O'er wife and child, to round about them weave
    And wind and bind them as one harvest-sheaf
Of love—to cleave to, and *forever* cleave. . . .
                Lord, I believe:
                    Help Thou mine unbelief.

We must believe—
Impelled since infancy to seek some clear
Fulfilment, still withheld all seekers here;—
For never have we seen perfection nor
The glory we are ever seeking for:

130

But we *have* seen—all mortal souls as one—
Have seen its *promise,* in the morning sun—
Its blest assurance, in the stars of night;—
The ever-dawning of the dark to light;—
The tears down-falling from all eyes that grieve—
   The eyes uplifting from all deeps of grief,
Yearning for what at last we shall receive.　.　.　.
              Lord, I believe:
                   Help Thou mine unbelief.

We must believe—
For still all unappeased our hunger goes,
From life's first waking, to its last repose:
The briefest life of any babe, or man
Outwearing even the allotted span,
Is each a life unfinished—incomplete:
For these, then, of th' outworn, or unworn feet
Denied one toddling step—　O there must be
Some fair, green, flowery pathway endlessly
Winding through lands Elysian! Lord, receive
   And lead each as Thine Own Child—even the Chief
Of us who didst Immortal life achieve.　.　.　.
              Lord, I believe:
                   Help Thou mine unbelief.

A GOOD MAN

I

A GOOD man never dies—
   In worthy deed and prayer
And helpful hands, and honest eyes,
   If smiles or tears be there:
Who lives for you and me—
   Lives for the world he tries
To help—he lives eternally.
   A good man never dies.

II

Who lives to bravely take
   His share of toil and stress,
And, for his weaker fellows' sake,
   Makes every burden less,—
He may, at last, seem worn—
   Lie fallen—hands and eyes
Folded—yet, though we mourn and mourn,
   A good man never dies.

THE OLD DAYS

THE old days—the far days—
The overdear and fair!—
The old days—the lost days—
How lovely they were!
The old days of Morning,
With the dew-drench on the flowers
And apple-buds and blossoms
Of those old days of ours.

Then was the *real* gold
   Spendthrift Summer flung;
Then was the *real* song
   Bird or Poet sung!
There was never censure then,—
   Only honest praise—
And all things were worthy of it
   In the old days.

There bide the true friends—
   The first and the best;
There clings the green grass
   Close where they rest:
Would they were here? No;—
   Would *we* were *there!* . . .
The old days—the lost days—
   How lovely they were!

A SPRING SONG AND A LATER

SHE sang a song of May for me,
    Wherein once more I heard
The mirth of my glad infancy—
    The orchard's earliest bird—
The joyous breeze among the trees
    New-clad in leaf and bloom,
And there the happy honey-bees
    In dewy gleam and gloom.

So purely, sweetly on the sense
    Of heart and spirit fell
Her song of Spring, its influence—
    Still irresistible,—
Commands me here—with eyes ablur—
    To mate her bright refrain,
Though I but shed a rhyme for her
    As dim as Autumn rain.

KNEELING WITH HERRICK

D EAR Lord, to Thee my knee is bent.—
         Give me content—
Full-pleasured with what comes to me,
         Whate'er it be:
An humble roof—a frugal board,
         And simple hoard;
The wintry fagot piled beside
         The chimney wide,
While the enwreathing flames up-sprout
         And twine about
The brazen dogs that guard my hearth
         And household worth:
Tinge with the ember's ruddy glow
         The rafters low;
And let the sparks snap with delight,
         As fingers might
That mark deft measures of some tune
         The children croon:
Then, with good friends, the rarest few
         Thou holdest true,
Ranged round about the blaze, to share
         My comfort there,—
Give me to claim the service meet
         That makes each seat
A place of honor, and each guest
         Loved as the rest.

THE RAINY MORNING

T HE dawn of the day was dreary,
    And the lowering clouds o'erhead
Wept in a silent sorrow
    Where the sweet sunshine lay dead;
And a wind came out of the eastward
    Like an endless sigh of pain,
And the leaves fell down in the pathway
    And writhed in the falling rain.

I had tried in a brave endeavor
   To chord my harp with the sun,
But the strings would slacken ever,
   And the task was a weary one:
And so, like a child impatient
   And sick of a discontent,
I bowed in a shower of teardrops
   And mourned with the instrument.

And lo! as I bowed, the splendor
   Of the sun bent over me,
With a touch as warm and tender
   As a father's hand might be:
And even as I felt its presence,
   My clouded soul grew bright,
And the tears, like the rain of morning,
   Melted in mists of light.

REACH YOUR HAND TO ME

REACH your hand to me, my friend,
  With its heartiest caress—
Sometime there will come an end
  To its present faithfulness—
    Sometime I may ask in vain
    For the touch of it again,
    When between us land or sea
    Holds it ever back from me.

Sometime I may need it so,
　　Groping somewhere in the night,
It will seem to me as though
　　Just a touch, however light,
　　　　Would make all the darkness day,
　　　　And along some sunny way
　　　　Lead me through an April-shower
　　　　Of my tears to this fair hour.

O the present is too sweet
　　To go on forever thus!
Round the corner of the street
　　Who can say what waits for us?—
　　　　Meeting—greeting, night and day,
　　　　Faring each the selfsame way—
　　　　Still somewhere the path must end.—
　　　　Reach your hand to me, my friend!

TO MY OLD FRIEND, WILLIAM LEACHMAN

FER forty year and better you have been a friend
 to me,
Through days of sore afflictions and dire adversity,
You allus had a kind word of counsul to impart,
Which was like a healin' 'intment to the sorrow of my
 hart.

When I burried my first womern, William Leachman,
 it was you
Had the only consolation that I could listen to—
Fer I knowed you had gone through it and had rallied
 from the blow,
And when you said I'd do the same, I knowed you'd
 ort to know.

But that time I'll long remember; how I wundered
    here and thare—
Through the settin'-room and kitchen, and out in the
    open air—
And the snowflakes whirlin', whirlin', and the fields a
    frozen glare,
And the neghbors' sleds and wagons congergatin'
    ev'rywhare.

I turned my eyes to'rds heaven, but the sun was hid
    away;
I turned my eyes to'rds earth again, but all was cold
    and gray;
And the clock, like ice a-crackin', clickt the icy hours
    in two—
And my eyes'd never thawed out ef it hadn't been fer
    you!

We set thare by the smoke-house—me and you out
    thare alone—
Me a-thinkin'—you a-talkin' in a soothin' undertone—
You a-talkin'—me a-thinkin' of the summers long ago,
And a-writin' "Marthy—Marthy" with my finger in
    the snow!

William Leachman, I can see you jest as plane as I
      could then;
And your hand is on my shoulder, and you rouse me up
      again,
And I see the tears a-drippin' from your own eyes, as
      you say:
"Be rickonciled and bear it—we but linger fer a day!"

At the last Old Settlers' Meetin' we went j'intly, you
      and me—
Your hosses and my wagon, as you wanted it to be;
And sence I can remember, from the time we've negh-
      bored here,
In all sich friendly actions you have double-done your
      sheer.

It was better than the meetin', too, that nine-mile talk
      we had
Of the times when we first settled here and travel was
      so bad;
When we had to go on hoss-back, and sometimes on
      "Shanks's mare,"
And "blaze" a road fer them behind that had to travel
      thare.

149

And now we was a-trottin' 'long a level gravel pike,
In a big two-hoss road-wagon, jest as easy as you like—
Two of us on the front seat, and our wimmern-folks
      behind,
A-settin' in theyr Winsor-cheers in perfect peace of
      mind!

And we pinted out old landmarks, nearly faded out of
      sight:—
Thare they ust to rob the stage-coach; thare Gash Mor-
      gan had the fight
With the old stag-deer that pronged him—how he
      battled fer his life,
And lived to prove the story by the handle of his knife.

Thare the first griss-mill was put up in the Settlement,
      and we
Had tuck our grindin' to it in the Fall of Forty-three—
When we tuck our rifles with us, techin' elbows all the
      way,
And a-stickin' right together ev'ry minute, night and
      day.

150

Thare ust to 'stand the tavern that they called the
    "Travelers' Rest,"
And thare, beyent the covered bridge, "The Counter-
    fitters' Nest"—
Whare they claimed the house was ha'nted—that a
    man was murdered thare,
And burried underneath the floor, er 'round the place
    somewhare.

And the old Plank-road they laid along in Fifty-one er
    two—
You know we talked about the times when that old
    road was new:
How "Uncle Sam" put down that road and never taxed
    the State
Was a problem, don't you rickollect, we couldn't *dim-*
    onstrate?

Ways was devius, William Leachman, that me and you
    has past;
But as I found you true at first, I find you true at last;
And, now the time's a-comin' mighty nigh our jurney's
    end,
I want to throw wide open all my soul to you, my
    friend.

153

With the stren'th of all my bein', and the heat of hart
    and brane,
And ev'ry livin' drop of blood in artery and vane,
I love you and respect you, and I venerate your name,
Fer the name of William Leachman and True Man-
    hood's jest the same!

A BACKWARD LOOK

A S I sat smoking, alone, yesterday,
     And lazily leaning back in my chair,
Enjoying myself in a general way—
Allowing my thoughts a holiday
     From weariness, toil and care,—
My fancies—doubtless, for ventilation—
     Left ajar the gates of my mind,—
And Memory, seeing the situation,
     Slipped out in street of "Auld Lang Syne."

Wandering ever with tireless feet
     Through scenes of silence, and jubilee
Of long-hushed voices; and faces sweet
Were thronging the shadowy side of the street
     As far as the eye could see;
Dreaming again, in anticipation,
     The same old dreams of our boyhood's days
That never come true, from the vague sensation
     Of walking asleep in the world's strange ways.

Away to the house where I was born!
   And there was the selfsame clock that ticked
From the close of dusk to the burst of morn,
When life-warm hands plucked the golden corn
   And helped when the apples were picked.
And the "chany-dog" on the mantel-shelf,
   With the gilded collar and yellow eyes,
Looked just as at first, when I hugged myself
   Sound asleep with the dear surprise.

And down to the swing in the locust tree,
   Where the grass was worn from the trampled ground
And where "Eck" Skinner, "Old" Carr, and three
Or four such other boys used to be
   Doin' "sky-scrapers," or "whirlin' round:"
And again Bob climbed for the bluebird's nest,
   And again "had shows" in the buggy-shed
Of Guymon's barn, where still, unguessed,
   The old ghosts romp through the best days dead!

And again I gazed from the old school-room
   With a wistful look of a long June day,
When on my cheek was the hectic bloom
Caught of Mischief, as I presume—
   He had such a "partial" way,

It seemed, toward me.—And again I thought
    Of a probable likelihood to be
Kept in after school—for a girl was caught
    Catching a note from me.

And down through the woods to the swimming-hole—
    Where the big, white, hollow, old sycamore grows,—
And we never cared when the water was cold,
And always "ducked" the boy that told
    On the fellow that tied the clothes.—
When life went so like a dreamy rhyme,
    That it seems to me now that then
The world was having a jollier time
    Than it ever will have again.

150

AT SEA

O WE go down to sea in ships—
    But Hope remains behind,
And Love, with laughter on his lips,
    And Peace, of passive mind;
While out across the deeps of night,
    With lifted sails of prayer,
We voyage off in quest of light,
    Nor find it anywhere.

O Thou who wroughtest earth and sea,
    Yet keepest from our eyes
The shores of an eternity
    In calms of Paradise,
Blow back upon our foolish quest
    With all the driving rain
Of blinding tears and wild unrest,
    And waft us home again.

THE OLD GUITAR

NEGLECTED now is the old guitar
 And moldering into decay;
Fretted with many a rift and scar
 That the dull dust hides away,
While the spider spins a silver star
 In its silent lips to-day.

The keys hold only nerveless strings—
 The sinews of brave old airs
Are pulseless now; and the scarf that clings
 So closely here declares
A sad regret in its ravelings
 And the faded hue it wears.

But the old guitar, with a lenient grace,
 Has cherished a smile for me;
And its features hint of a fairer face
 That comes with a memory
Of a flower-and-perfume-haunted place
 And a moonlit balcony.

Music sweeter than words confess
 Or the minstrel's powers invent,
Thrilled here once at the light caress
 Of the fairy hands that lent
This excuse for the kiss I press
 On the dear old instrument.

The rose of pearl with the jeweled stem
 Still blooms; and the tiny sets
In the circle all are here; the gem
 In the keys, and the silver frets;
But the dainty fingers that danced o'er them—
 Alas for the heart's regrets!—

Alas for the loosened strings to-day,
 And the wounds of rift and scar
On a worn old heart, with its roundelay
 Enthralled with a stronger bar
That Fate weaves on, through a dull decay
 Like that of the old guitar!

JOHN McKEEN

JOHN McKEEN, in his rusty dress,
  His loosened collar, and swarthy throat;
His face unshaven, and none the less,
His hearty laugh and his wholesomeness,
  And the wealth of a workman's vote!

Bring him, O Memory, here once more,
  And tilt him back in his Windsor chair
By the kitchen-stove, when the day is o'er
And the light of the hearth is across the floor,
  And the crickets everywhere!

And let their voices be gladly blent
   With a watery jingle of pans and spoons,
And a motherly chirrup of sweet content,
And neighborly gossip and merriment,
    And old-time fiddle-tunes!

Tick the clock with a wooden sound,
   And fill the hearing with childish glee
Of rhyming riddle, or story found
In the Robinson Crusoe, leather-bound
    Old book of the Used-to-be!

John McKeen of the Past! Ah, John,
   To have grown ambitious in worldly ways!—
To have rolled your shirt-sleeves down, to don
A broadcloth suit, and, forgetful, gone
    Out on election days!

John, ah, John! did it prove your worth
   To yield you the office you still maintain?
To fill your pockets, but leave the dearth
Of all the happier things on earth
    To the hunger of heart and brain?

Under the dusk of your villa trees,
    Edging the drives where your blooded span
Paw the pebbles and wait your ease,—
Where are the children about your knees,
    And the mirth, and the happy man?

The blinds of your mansion are battened to;
    Your faded wife is a close recluse;
And your "finished" daughters will doubtless do
Dutifully all that is willed of you,
    And marry as you shall choose!—

But O for the old-home voices, blent
    With the watery jingle of pans and spoons,
And the motherly chirrup of glad content,
And neighborly gossip and merriment,
    And the old-time fiddle-tunes!

THROUGH SLEEPY-LAND

WHERE do you go when you go to sleep,
    Little Boy! Little Boy! where?
'Way—'way in where's Little Bo-Peep,
And Little Boy Blue, and the Cows and Sheep
    A-wandering 'way in there—in there—
      A-wandering 'way in there!

And what do you see when lost in dreams,
    Little Boy, 'way in there?
Firefly-glimmers and glowworm-gleams,
And silvery, low, slow-sliding streams,
    And mermaids, smiling out—'way in where
      They're a-hiding—'way in there!

Where do you go when the Fairies call,
   Little Boy! Little Boy! where?
Wade through the dews of the grasses tall,
Hearing the weir and the waterfall
   And the Wee Folk—'way in there—in there—
      And the Kelpies—'way in there!

And what do you do when you wake at dawn,
   Little Boy! Little Boy! what?
Hug my Mommy and kiss her on
Her smiling eyelids, sweet and wan,
   And tell her everything I've forgot
   About, a-wandering 'way in there—
      Through the blind-world 'way in there!

"THEM OLD CHEERY WORDS"

PAP he allus ust to say,
    "Chris'mus comes but onc't a year!"
Liked to hear him that-a-way,
    In his old split-bottomed cheer
By the fireplace here at night—
Wood all in,—and room all bright,
Warm and snug, and folks all here:
"Chris'mus comes but onc't a year!"

Me and 'Lize, and Warr'n and Jess
    And Eldory home fer two
Weeks' vacation; and, I guess,
    Old folks tickled through and through,
Same as *we* was,—"Home onc't more
Fer another Chris'mus—shore!"
Pap 'u'd say, and tilt his cheer,—
"Chris'mus comes but onc't a year!"

Mostly Pap was ap' to be
    Ser'ous in his "daily walk,"
As he called it; giner'ly
    Was no hand to joke er talk.
Fac's is, Pap had never be'n
Rugged-like at all—and then
Three years in the army had
Hepped to break him purty bad.

172

Never *flinched!* but frost and snow
   Hurt his wownd in winter.   But
You bet *Mother* knowed it, though!—
   Watched his feet, and made him putt
On his flannen; and his knee,
Where it never healed up, he
Claimed was "well now—mighty near—
Chris'mus comes but onc't a year!"

"Chris'mus comes but onc't a year!"
   Pap 'u'd say, and snap his eyes . . .
Row o' apples sputter'n' here
   Round the hearth, and me and 'Lize
Crackin' hicker'-nuts; and Warr'n
And Eldory parchin' corn;
And whole raft o' young folks here.
"Chris'mus comes but onc't a year!"

Mother tuk most comfort in
   Jest a-heppin' Pap: She'd fill
His pipe fer him, er his tin
   O' hard cider; er set still
And read fer him out the pile
O' newspapers putt on file
Whilse he was with Sherman—(She
Knowed the whole war-history!)

175

"THEM OLD CHEERY WORDS"

Sometimes he'd git het up some.—
   "Boys," he'd say, "and you girls, too,
Chris'mus is about to come;
   So, as you've a right to do,
Celebrate it! Lots has died,
Same as Him they crucified,
That you might be happy here.
Chris'mus comes but onc't a year!"

Missed his voice last Chris'mus—missed
   Them old cheery words, you know.
Mother helt up tel she kissed
   All of us—then had to go
And break down! And I laughs: "Here!
'Chris'mus comes but onc't a year!'"
"Them's his very words," sobbed she,
"When he asked to marry me."

"Chris'mus comes but onc't a year!"
   "Chris'mus comes but onc't a year!"
Over, over, still I hear,
   "Chris'mus comes but onc't a year!"
Yit, like him, I'm goin' to smile
And keep cheerful all the while:
Allus Chris'mus *There*—And here
"Chris'mus comes but onc't a year!"

TO THE JUDGE

A Voice From the Interior of Old Hoop-Pole Township

FRIEND of my earliest youth,
    Can't you arrange to come down
And visit a fellow out here in the woods—
    Out of the dust of the town?
Can't you forget you're a Judge
    And put by your dolorous frown
And tan your wan face in the smile of a friend—
    Can't you arrange to come down?

Can't you forget for a while
    The arguments prosy and drear,—
To lean at full-length in indefinite rest
    In the lap of the greenery here?
Can't you kick over "the Bench,"
    And "husk" yourself out of your gown
To dangle your legs where the fishing is good—
    Can't you arrange to come down?

Bah! for your office of State!
    And bah! for its technical lore!
What does our President, high in his chair,
    But wish himself low as before!
Pick between peasant and king,—
    Poke your bald head through a crown
Or shadow it here with the laurels of Spring!—
    Can't you arrange to come down?

"Judge it" out *here,* if you will,—
    The birds are in session by dawn;
You can draw, not *complaints,* but a sketch of the hill
    And a breath that your betters have drawn;
You can open your heart, like a case,
    To a jury of kine, white and brown,
And their verdict of "Moo" will just satisfy you!—
    Can't you arrange to come down?

Can't you arrange it, old Pard?—
   Pigeonhole Blackstone and Kent!—
Here we have "Breitmann," and Ward,
   Twain, Burdette, Nye, and content!
Can't you forget you're a Judge
   And put by your dolorous frown
And tan your wan face in the smile of a friend—
   Can't you arrange to come down?

OUR BOYHOOD HAUNTS

HO! I'm going back to where
 We were youngsters.—Meet me there,
Dear old barefoot chum, and we
Will be as we used to be,—
Lawless rangers up and down
The old creek beyond the town—
Little sunburnt gods at play,
Just as in that far-away:—
Water nymphs, all unafraid,
Shall smile at us from the brink
Of the old millrace and wade
Tow'rd us as we kneeling drink
At the spring our boyhood knew,
Pure and clear as morning-dew:

And, as we are rising there,
Doubly dow'rd to hear and see,
We shall thus be made aware
Of an eerie piping, heard
High above the happy bird
In the hazel: And then we,
Just across the creek, shall see
(Hah! the goaty rascal!) Pan
Hoof it o'er the sloping green,
Mad with his own melody,
Aye, and (bless the beasty man!)
Stamping from the grassy soil
Bruiséd scents of *fleur-de-lis,*
Boneset, mint and pennyroyal.

MY DANCIN'-DAYS IS OVER

WHAT is it in old fiddle-chunes 'at makes me ketch
        my breath
And ripples up my backbone tel I'm tickled most to
        death?—
    Kindo' like that sweet-sick feelin', in the long sweep
        of a swing,
    The first you ever swung in, with yer first sweet-
        heart, i jing!—
    Yer first picnic—yer first ice-cream—yer first o'
    ever'thing
        'At happened 'fore yer dancin'-days wuz over!

I never understood it—and I s'pose I never can,—
But right in town here, yisterd'y, I heerd a pore blind-
        man
    A-fiddlin' old "Gray Eagle"—*And*-sir! I jes
        stopped my load
    O' hay and listened at him—yes, and watched the
        way he "bow'd,"—
    And back I went, plum forty year', with boys and
        girls I knowed
        And loved, long 'fore my dancin'-days wuz
        over!—

At high noon in yer city,—with yer blame Magnetic-
    Cars
A-hummin' and a-screetchin' past—and bands and G.
    A. R.'s
  A-marchin'—and fire-ingines.—*All* the noise, the
      whole street through,
  Wuz lost on me!—I only heerd a whipperwill er two,
  It 'peared-like, kindo' callin' 'crost the darkness and
      the dew,
    Them nights afore my dancin'-days wuz over.

T'uz Chused'y-night at Wetherell's, er We'nsd'y-night
    at Strawn's,
Er Fourth-o'-July-night at uther Tomps's house er
    John's!—
  With old Lew Church from Sugar Crick, with that
      old fiddle he
  Had sawed clean through the Army, from Atlanty
      to the sea—
  And yit he'd fetched her home ag'in, so's he could
      play fer me
    Onc't more afore my dancin'-days wuz over!

The woods 'at's all ben cut away wuz growin' same as
    then;
The youngsters all wuz boys ag'in 'at's now all oldish
    men;
    And all the girls 'at *then* wuz girls—I saw 'em, one
      and all,
    As *plain* as then—the middle-sized, the short-and-
      fat, and tall—
    And, 'peared-like, I danced "Tucker" fer 'em up and
      down the wall
      Jes like afore my dancin' days wuz over!

        .   .   .   .   .   .

Yer *po*-leece they can holler "Say! *you,* Uncle! drive
    ahead!—
You can't use *all* the right-o'-way!"—fer that wuz
    what they said!—
    But, jes the same,—in spite of all 'at you call "inter-
      prise
    And prog-gress of *you*-folks Today," we're all of
      fambly-ties—
    We're all got feelin's fittin' fer the *tears* 'at's in our
      eyes
      Er the *smiles* afore our dancin'-days is over.

HER BEAUTIFUL HANDS

O YOUR hands—they are strangely fair!
    Fair—for the jewels that sparkle there,—
Fair—for the witchery of the spell
That ivory keys alone can tell;
But when their delicate touches rest
Here in my own do I love them best,
As I clasp with eager acquisitive spans
My glorious treasure of beautiful hands!

Marvelous—wonderful—beautiful hands!
They can coax roses to bloom in the strands
Of your brown tresses; and ribbons will twine,
Under mysterious touches of thine,
Into such knots as entangle the soul,
And fetter the heart under such a control
As only the strength of my love understands—
My passionate love for your beautiful hands.

As I remember the first fair touch
Of those beautiful hands that I love so much,
I seem to thrill as I then was thrilled,
Kissing the glove that I found unfilled—
When I met your gaze, and the queenly bow,
As you said to me, laughingly, "Keep it now!"
And dazed and alone in a dream I stand
Kissing this ghost of your beautiful hand.

When first I loved, in the long ago,
And held your hand as I told you so—
Pressed and caressed it and gave it a kiss,
And said "I could die for a hand like this!"
Little I dreamed love's fulness yet
Had to ripen when eyes were wet,
And prayers were vain in their wild demands
For one warm touch of your beautiful hands.

Beautiful Hands! O Beautiful Hands!
Could you reach out of the alien lands
Where you are lingering, and give me, to-night,
Only a touch—were it ever so light—
My heart were soothed, and my weary brain
Would lull itself into rest again;
For there is no solace the world commands
Like the caress of your beautiful hands.